a decade

samm joyy

Published in Canada by Engen Books, Chapel Arm, NL.

Library and Archives Canada Cataloguing in Publication information is available on the publisher's website.

ISBN-13: 978-1-77478-157-9

Distributed by:
Engen Books
www.engenbooks.com
submissions@engenbooks.com

First mass market paperback printing: April 2024

Cover Image: Engen Books

a decade

samm joyy

ENGEN
BOOKS

For those who are struggling.

October 9, 2012

For years the adults asked us
what we wanted to be when we grew up
and we answered with the plainest jobs;
the only ones we knew of.

I'm going to be a veterinarian,
a doctor, a firefighter, a teacher.
I'm going to be a mommy, like my mommy.

We believed we'd get a job like our parents,
fall in love and never get hurt,
repopulate the earth with little babies —
ones that didn't cry or crave attention.

We imagined living in big houses, with windows
that held the deepest views
of oceans, or trees, or big cities with lights
and driving fancy cars, or mini vans or motorcycles like our dads.

Paying for everything with plastic cards, and money would be free
and we'd have enough quarters for every selection
in the candy machines.

When we were five there was no such thing as;
alcoholism and drug addiction,
STIs and HIV, abortion and teen pregnancy.
Our minds were unable to see the reality
what would await us when we grew
student debt and IOUs, rent, car and insurance due
working two jobs and it's still hard to make payments
This is not what we wanted then, if only we knew.

Someone asked me the other day
what I want to be when I'm done school
A journalist was my first reply
But other than that I said,
I hope I'm still alive.

June 15, 2013

An Excerpt

She downed the beer as if it was her only means of survival. The cold, crisp wetness hit her lips and she felt an ease, a safety. The bartender smiled at her. She wondered if he had any idea who she was or if he even cared.

She rocked back and forth on the wobbly bar stool. Her body was slowly giving up on her. Painfully. Physically she was nearing the end, but her mind kept her going. The longer she was inebriated, the longer she could go without remembering. The bottle kept her calm, sane. It assured her that there was happiness out there. Whether or not it was real, she didn't care. Any state of happiness was better than the lifelong state of depression she had been living.

October 23, 2013

I hate the wondering.
What color would her eyes have been?
Would she light up when she smiled?
That's something I haven't done in a while.
I hate the wondering.
What kind of person would she be?
Would she look more like mom or dad?
Would she appreciate the life she's never had?
I hate the wondering.
Six feet under in a porcelain white dress,
a daughter, a sister
God damn I miss her.

February 8, 2014

It fills my lungs
until my chest is tight.
A feeling that I never
felt was right,
until now –
I hadn't thought
of this before.
It was always one man and
then one more.
now I'm fine
with You and I
and This.
All I needed was a simple kiss
upon my forehead,
and an arm around my waist
Just a taste –
of something I could not deserve.
You place a finger on my lips
and say, "not another word".
So, I shut my mouth and
close my eyes and agree to try.

February 18, 2014

I was the light
Shining down on the stage
Blinding your sight
As you turned the page

I was the sound
You made into a song
As your words spun around
They strung me along

I was the air
Your chest would ignore
I stripped myself bare
But you wanted more

I was the rain
You'd pretend not to feel
An escape from the pain
An escape from what's real.

March 27, 2014

Surrounded by strangers in a strange bar, she searched for a familiar face, but the booze blinded her.

Like a rehearsed routine, she sacrificed her sleep for his company.
Tonight however, he was nowhere to be found. He had made his
easy escape, clean cut, painless
For him at least.

Regret eroded her mind. It had been years since she let vulnerability back into her vocabulary, but he managed to seduce her into speaking. With no desire to re-enact the lifestyle she had before music notes mesmerized her mind, she couldn't help but feel nostalgic for the night life.

The very thought of complete control made her heart race.
The desire to be wanted, to feel desirable.
She had that power once; he had let her feel that way once.
a relationship built under blankets, strengthened by substance,
and nurtured only by nightfall.

As sunrise seeped through the curtains, a hand shielded blood shot eyes; her face merely a mirage. She would leave her scent on the pillow and a glass of water on the table, proof that she was there with no obligation to ever return.

"Leave before you're left." She savored the thought in her mind endlessly.
And then it hit her.
He had left.

August 10, 2014

My lipstick stains your skin,
rib cage of steel won't let you in.
An ice-cold heart, a soul of sin
Just stop now, this cannot begin.
A dreaded disease in disguise
Hourglass model, doe eyes.
I awake when the stars rise
My alarm clock mimics your cries.
Sweet breath of berry wine
Please believe me, I'm fine.
Just balancing on a thin line
between insanity
and what's really mine.
Nothing for me to defend
When your back breaks, mine bends.
Please don't confuse the message I send
Where your body starts, mine ends.

October 26, 2014

If secrets are for sinners
send me straight to hell
They say the truth can hurt
so I guess I might as well
join the alcoholics
and pour myself a drink
Life is always easier
when you don't have to think
about tomorrow
or the days within the past
Empty the bottles baby
so this innocence can last

November 20, 2014

Throughout my body
numbness lingers
as I retrace the marks
left by your fingers

They remind me of a time
I wish not to speak of
when bruises would measure
the extent of his love

A point in my life where
my future was bleak
because under his hands
I was fragile and weak

However, it seems
when you leave them
I feel –
I feel like these bruises
prove that I'm real

You left them in lust
marks in anger he made
I'll be scarred forever
even after they fade

Date Unknown

I'm afraid of my own mind
while my family is afraid to find
my body consumed by darkness
I hide what I want to confess
that I'm afraid to die by my own hand
If I can't, how will they understand–
That I drink to feel something besides sad
Why can't I seize the happiness I once had?

January 12, 2015

Lost without a map,
stuck within this trap
I call my mind.
I swear I'm fine
I lied.
The voices are so loud,
I cannot hear a sound.
I have no compass to direct me
this disease continues to infect me,
Why did life select me?
Was this fate or simply stupidity?

April 26, 2015

I sit here and think
as I try not to blink
while you ejaculate
your thoughts all over my face

my heart can bare
anything your mouth
can spit at me

I've been gagged and whipped
by emotions unrequited
I have learned the hard way
to try not to fight it

So I wipe my face clean
and redress myself with pride
keep my feelings to myself
because I cannot seem to hide

Date Unknown

Her heart beat faster than the rain fell
It was hard to keep her body still.
Eyes barely set in their sockets
a noise in her brain sounded like
loose change in her pockets.

Trembled and unsteady she shook
afraid to move, unable to look.
He stood barely a foot away
Her conscience wanted her to run,
her body ached for her to stay.

She could hear his lungs fill with air
then collapse while he moved near
All at once she fell apart
he took her hand and stopped her heart.
Still avoiding direct eye contact
She wondered how she would react
he had caused her significant pain,
left on her soul an inevitable stain.

His breath heavy with whiskey
almost strong enough to see
lingered by her ear, almost gracefully.
Seduced by the scent he was aware what it meant

July 15, 2015

His bare skin
hidden beneath covers
we make love
but do not love one another

His soul and sin
naked here beside me
goosebumps on my skin
as his hands explore my body

I crave him
as a temporary happiness
an unspoken rule
we want nothing more and nothing less

Limb by limb
we have both been here before
cloaked in cigarettes and sweat
our clothes lay on the floor

We shake hands
when our business deal is done
Both parties satisfied
continue to the next one

Date Unknown

Patience
is holding my tongue while you bitch about how she treats you

Patience
is waiting until four in the morning when you need a ride home

Patience
is staying home waiting for a call, but two hours have passed, and my phone hasn't rang

Patience
is chain smoking outside the restaurant you said we should meet at

Patience
is waking up early to drive you to work but you slept in

Patience
is rubbing your back while you puke because you drank for nine hours straight

Patience
is putting my plans on hold because you're sad and want to see me

Patience
is lying to my friends about you

Patience is a virtue that I wish I didn't have

January 16, 2017

Secrets:

"Let's keep this between you and I."
"No one will believe you if you tell."
"Keep your mouth shut and everything will be fine."
"What she doesn't know can't hurt her."
"You're good at keeping secrets, right?"
"I'm not ashamed or anything, I just don't want anyone to find out."
"I don't want my friends to know."
"Let's pretend this didn't happen."
"I don't want to get into trouble, so just keep quiet."
"We don't want people to suspect things."
"I don't want you to get attached."
"This will be quick and painless."
"I just need you to get me off and go home."

Date Unknown

To feel the chill in her skin
to touch her would be to sin.
To see where she has been to
to love her would kill you.
To smell the scent of her hair
to taste her if you dare.
To hear the words she has to say
do you leave or do you stay?

February 16, 2017

When you kept me inside
I took it as protection

And when you would not speak to me
I took it as connection

When you pushed that burning flame into my arm
I took it as an addition to my complexion

And when you held me down to have your way
I took it as affection

You took away my personality
And my ability to perceive the situation

You became apart of me
Incurable infection

And after everything you put me though

When you left
I took it as rejection

May 24, 2017

For years I bitched and complained
about all the men and all the names
They'd call me
easy, sleazy
tight pussy like no man's fucked before
but she's a whore
so I tapped out
sworn off the sex–
–ual frustration
couldn't handle the infatuations
anymore

When love is just lust with white lies
how do you tell the difference
how do you stop the cry–
–ing and now I'm sighing
because I've put myself in this position
passion without a paycheck
Reality check or constitution

A world in which my body is the whole of me
and my education was a failure
so it no longer serves a purpose
and my skill with words just makes for
more
Desired dirty talk than anything
more than surface
value
that V word stings
more than virginity

But the man I lost mine to
was a king and he moved away
to become some celebrity
He left me alone
in this bewildering city
where people work all week
making money to spend on George Street

Get intoxicating,
grinding at KFuse
is the new form of mating
In the daytime
we sit in coffee shops
snapping Insta-shots of our coffee grinds
as if it's a form of art
I can't believe he left me torn apart
living in a city called Paradise
where the traffic is backed up for three sets of lights
and the potholes are moon craters
soon enough I'll need an excavator
to help remove my Kia from the damn holes
And some people have said
Why don't you go and move
G.T.F.O
And I did once, packed up my shit
and drove to Halifax
where the waterfront was nicer
but I only lasted two months there
because I fell for a boy
whose best friend fell for me
and that monogamous relationship
turned into a ship of three

Jealousy is a hard monster to kill
when your boyfriend is okay
with you sleeping with his best friend but you can't handle him
sexting another woman.

February 18, 2021

Wrap the towel tighter
dry off and cover up
try not to get lost in the reflection
of a body that doesn't feel like yours

The scars have healed
but some wounds never go away
his knife may have been removed
yet it still keeps stabbing

Sometimes it is subtle
a migraine of memories
Other times it is chaotic
impaling your mind

Are you driving? Pull over.
A stab like that will send you off the edge
At a bar? Go home.
You know pain can be subdued if you dilute it.

February 18, 2021

A spotlight on your face
Your phone glowing in the dark
Lit room we share–
a bed, two chargers,
four walls stand around us
a dream between
two people barely living
imagining a life of grandeur
accepting what we have
or the door.

Preoccupied by the attention
of online lovers,
followers, camera shutters
capture the moment
in an instant
but do they capture the discontent
the wall of debt, the secrets kept.
Glued to the glow - the glamour
post coital, pre cuddle
fall into your phone
instant enamor
are these hormones
or screen scrolls.

February 18, 2021

I cannot exist
in a world where I am silenced
because I don't agree
This conversation is not a kink
I'm willing to try
Stop trying to gag me

Paint the letter A on my chest
but not for adulterous
Leave it for the anger in me
and the audacity you have

Believing that this world can be perfect
if I keep my mind to myself
there's no need for anyone to hear
the voice of a woman in conflict

Place my opinion upon the shelf
bring my body to the gallows
to hang with the Northern Star

Someday you'll be sheared
following the herd
like the sheep you are

February 18, 2021

It was a fleeting feeling
the sudden untangle of fingers
warm embrace turned cold shoulder

Slipped on your shoes
eyes straight to the floor
didn't leave enough time
for the door to hit you

on the way out
It was no movie scene
no profound regret
no looking back

And as I watched
the sedan speed off
from the bay window
I wondered
why I didn't feel anything
at all.

February 18, 2021

Sip sip sipping
on your smile of gin
and dreaming of
blue skies

Your blue eyes
look in
through the window
I look out

No rainbows in the bar
sweat and steamy lust
Romance doesn't stand
a chance
between two strangers

Dancing on creaky
Floorboards
Floorboards
Keep us from falling
on our face

In a love that
embraces the burn
of the shots we swallow
and the ones we miss

May 29, 2021

Dreaded disease in disguise
hour glass model, doe eyes
If you ask me – I'm fine
just balancing on a thin line
between reality and what's really mine

The sobriety is making me
rethink who I am
and I understand
that my baggage is a lot to carry

So I burned all emotions unrequited
and I don't dare fight it
there are too many eyes of pity
in the city
I once called home

I dug up the roots I planted
and took them with me
repotted my lifestyle
into something a little more worthwhile

And if you ask me – I'm fine
just balancing on a thin line
of sobriety
because beer was always there
when you were not

And I forgot for a minute who I was
until those eyes looked right through me
pulled me deeper
made me sit and look in the mirror
at who I've become

One disease down
one to go
take it slow
on the highway
trees on both sides

If you ask me – I'm fine
just balancing on a thin line
between East and West
and if I were to guess
this is the best decision I could have made

Although I'm afraid
to get too close
to something I don't know
I'm feeling all my feelings
out in the open
want to shove them all back in
and begin
again

June 13, 2021

The past seven nights
I've cried myself to sleep
but don't take pity on me
while I weep

I swear
I'm not trying to die
by my own hand
whether from liquor or locket
kitchen or pocket

I keep trying to place
all those behind
think with a clear mind
but that's hard to come by
when my thoughts fly

through every red light
and stop sign
driving too fast
too close to that yellow line

December 5, 2021

I am eleven months sober
but all I want is a beer
One sip is all it would take
to fall back in, I swear

How can I be too much
and yet not enough

The Author

Samm Joyy is a poet born, raised, and living in St. John's, Newfoundland.

One of the most brilliant young authors of her time, Joyy helped run the Spoken Word St. John's (SWSJ) poetry scene from 2014-2022. In 2022 she edited *The Birds Come Back in the Spring*, the debut poetry collection from Hannah Jenkins.

Her poems focus on how one comes to grip with the darker aspects of one's own personality, grows to accept them, and eventually grows to feel comfortable showing them to the world. Her brutally honest work examines not only the poet but Newfoundland culture, touching on alcoholism, the arts, and downtown life.

www.ingramcontent.com/pod-product-compliance
Lightning Source LLC
Chambersburg PA
CBHW031221090426
42740CB00009B/1254